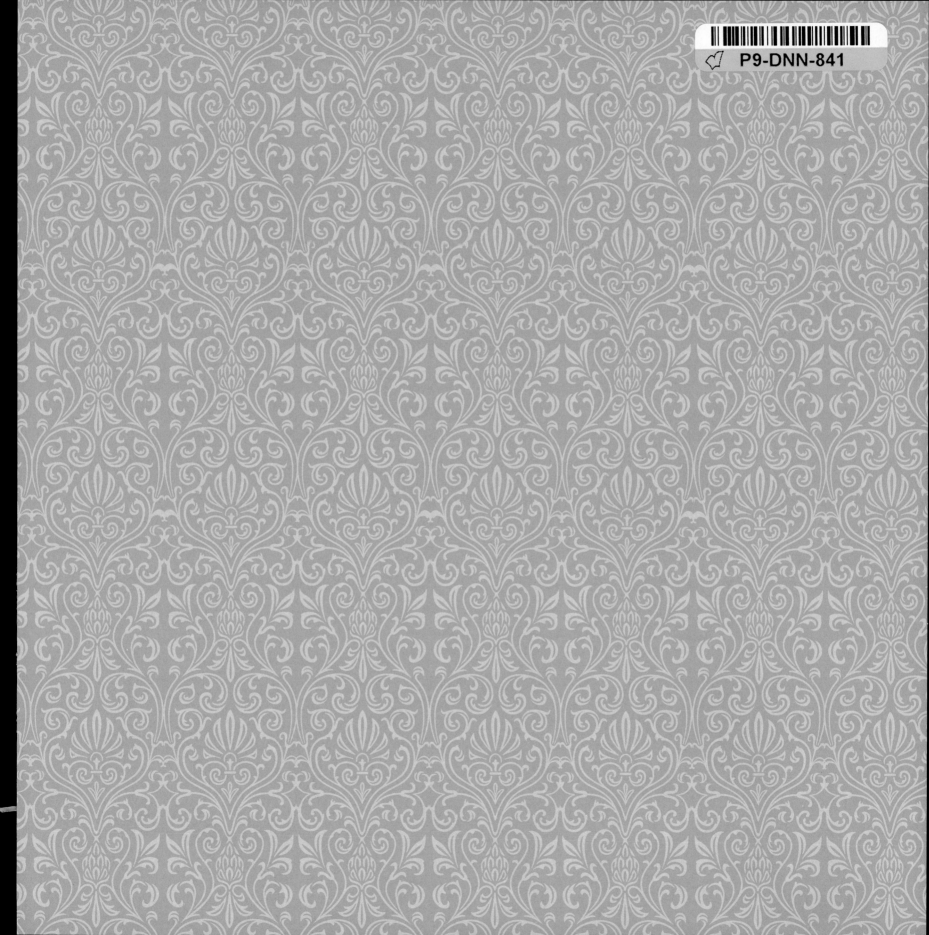

DOWNTOWN CHIC

DESIGNING YOUR DREAM HOME:

FROM WRECK TO RAVISHING

ROBERT AND CORTNEY NOVOGRATZ

WITH ELIZABETH NOVOGRATZ

RIZZOLI
NEW YORK

FOR HENI

We could not do any of this without you

First published in the United States in 2009 by
Rizzoli International Publications, Inc.
300 Park Avenue South
New York, NY 10010
www.rizzoliusa.com

2010 2011 2012 / 10 9 8 7 6 5 4 3 2
ISBN 13: 978-08478-3173-9

Library of Congress Control Number: 2008944143

Designed by Paul Kepple, Headcase Design

Printed in the United States

CHAPTER ONE

CHAPTER TWO

CHAPTER THREE

CHAPTER FOUR

CHAPTER FIVE

CHAPTER SIX

CHAPTER SEVEN

CHAPTER EIGHT

CHAPTER NINE

CONTENTS

PREFACE

I decided to put this book together because I am often asked how and why
my husband Robert and I do what we do—create amazing living spaces while
managing a brood of six kids under the age of eleven living in New York City.
My response has always been that it's what we love to do, so that helps make it
a bit easier; as for the "how," we usually wing it. Our passion is creating homes
for families that function well while looking great, and we love the mayhem
that is invariably part of that process. And while those reasons explain why
we decided to do what we do, I think the most important reason is this: a
home isn't just where you live, or at least it doesn't have to be. A home is who
you are. The houses that Robert and I have designed and built over the years
are testaments to what we've been through, representatives of the chapters
of our life together, and concrete proof that having faith in ourselves and one
another can accomplish great things. The houses we've built for ourselves
mean far more to us than just having a roof over our heads. They are an
expression of where we've been and all of the people that have been a part of
our lives. It was while building the houses that we wanted to live in that we
decided we could help others realize their own dream houses. Sure, this may
sound sentimental, but talk to anyone whose home truly represents who they
are and what they value, and they will tell you about the joy it brings them.
Believe me, that feeling can't be underestimated.

   Creating this book has been a gift. Its afforded us a chance to look back,
to relive and remember the joys, the mistakes, the many crises, and the
celebrations that were a part of each project. We hope that it will be helpful
or inspiring or even a "what not to do" manual for those who are renovating
a kitchen, redecorating a bedroom, or even building their first house. We
hope it will remind you that regardless of your home project, that you do it
with a sense of humor, allow yourself to learn from your mistakes, and most
importantly, enjoy every bit of it.

— *CORTNEY NOVOGRATZ*

Our wedding invitation painted by Pat Palomino, a close friend and talented artist. In the early days, we were always big on creativity but low on funds. We wanted a very personal wedding invitation, not something you pick up at your local stationers. So, we asked Pat to paint something for us. This began our tradition of creating one-of-a-kind holiday cards and invitations that are unique and don't break the bank (see Chapter 9, pg. 164, to see all of the cards we've created over the years).

INTRODUCTION

Fifteen years ago, my husband Robert and I got engaged and purchased our first home. The house was a condemned building in the middle of Chelsea, a once neglected neighborhood in downtown Manhattan that has since become very trendy. At the time, neither of us knew that buying and renovating this building would change our lives, igniting a passion that would sow the seeds for our future company. Since then, we have renovated and designed numerous buildings in and around New York City, including rebuilding an entire block in SoHo.

Robert and I were first introduced at a party in North Carolina. I was in college and he was working as a stockbroker. It was love at first sight, and a few months later I graduated and we both moved to New York. Over the next three years, Robert worked on Wall Street while I pursued an acting career, but we were both looking for something more fulfilling and exciting than our careers offered. It was quite a shock when we found what we were looking for in a dilapidated brownstone, and began to realize we'd found our calling. It probably shouldn't have

been such a surprise, though, as we both grew up with parents who loved antiques and were constantly renovating. Robert spent much of his childhood fascinated by architecture, while I spent much of mine involved in decorating—yes, even as a child I was constantly redoing my room and my siblings' rooms.

We bought the Chelsea building that April and were under full construction by May. At the same time, we were planning our wedding, which would take place in Georgia that June with five hundred guests. We were busy. Robert was also promoting parties in New York in those days, which helped ease the stress of the wedding, as we looked at it as just another big party. We figured as long as there were family, friends, good music, and a lot of alcohol, nothing could go too wrong. Aside from a few minor mishaps—forgetting to pick the priest up from the airport (which upset him so much that he flew back to New York before the ceremony), the cake catching on fire, a few cousins passing out in the neighbor's yard, and the police showing up—we had the time of our lives.

"I met a lot of people in Europe, I even encountered myself."

—JAMES BALDWIN

We spent our honeymoon in France, falling in love with the artifacts and antiques that we saw everywhere but couldn't afford. This was the beginning of our shared passion for looking around the world for great design ideas and finding interesting pieces to bring back home. Unfortunately, due to a lack of funds we returned home empty-handed and were met with the stress of renovating a condemned building on a shoestring budget. The honeymoon was over.

Neither of us knew anything about building, renovating, or construction, but, as we had very little money, we learned fast. We had a few things in our favor: we both loved the chaos, we didn't stress over the little things, and we worked well as a team. The only real problem was that we had absolutely no idea what we were doing.

We found lots of inspiration on our honeymoon, from the charming rustic facades to grand cherub sculptures. I think the one in this photograph (left) inspired us to use a cherub relief (right) on the facade of one of the houses we built on Thompson Street some years later (pg. 51).

"I saw the angel in the marble and carved
until I set him free."

—MICHELANGELO

:: CHAPTER ONE

"Trust your own instinct.
Your mistakes might as well be your
own instead of someone else's."

—BILLY WILDER

OUR FIRST HOUSE :: BEFORE

DISCOVERING FLEA MARKET CHIC

WHAT WE DID

:: Gut renovated a 150-year-old brownstone (salvaging only the staircase, front door, and fireplace) and transformed it into a two-family house, using the additional rental income to pay half of the mortgage.

:: Designed a house without an architect.

:: Rebuilt all of the beams.

:: Reframed the entire house.

:: Installed all new mechanicals (HVAC and plumbing).

:: Added a new roof, new windows, new everything.

:: Installed a stainless steel kitchen.

:: Repainted the entire interior and exterior.

:: Built a roof garden.

:: Decorated the entire house on a very strict budget using flea market finds.

:: Installed bathroom tile by ourselves, so badly it had to be ripped out.

:: Dreamt a lot about what the wreck could become.

"Every artist was first an amateur.

—RALPH WALDO EMERSON

THE
YELLOW
HOUSE

We painted the drab brownstone yellow to brighten up the block. Ever since, we haven't been able to get away from yellow—it pops up in one way or another in all of our projects. It's become our good luck color.

:: AFTER

"Arrange whatever pieces come your way."

—VIRGINIA WOOLF

THE FIRST STEPS

The house—located in Chelsea, a neighborhood in downtown Manhattan—looked like a bomb had hit it, but it had great bones. We had an engineer friend take a look at it, and he agreed that it looked terrible but that the structure and foundation were sound. This was all that was important. He also told us to get three bids for a contractor and to go with the middle bid. When the bids came in, we couldn't even afford the lowest bid. We ended up hiring Aaron, a twenty-two-year-old family friend and apprentice carpenter who'd just moved to New York. We took a chance on Aaron—he was young and so were we, so we figured it out as we went along, together.

Our next step was to find an architect. People suggested that we find a young, upstart firm, that they might be affordable. We found such a firm, and the first thing they wanted to do was measure the house, which would cost $12,000. Instead, we spent $2.99 on a tape measure and began our career as architects.

Our vision was to keep the house as open as possible. We assembled the demo crew: Aaron, Robert's little brother and his

friend, and the two of us. Nothing could be salvaged except the front door, the staircase, and the fireplace. We rented a garbage container, which cost $450 each time we filled it. The first night, pre-demo, the neighbors filled it with mattresses, old TVs, and trash. *Welcome to New York!* Ten days later, finally, we had an empty shell. The demo went well, meaning nothing collapsed and nobody died; although I came close one morning when I fell through the beams. Aaron promptly asked me to leave the job site, claiming that I was a danger to the crew and to myself.

I didn't leave and tried my best to stay out of trouble. Which I did until it was time to hire the cement guy to pour the basement floor. I found a guy named John Gotti (really) in the Yellow Pages. He wanted to get paid before he finished the job, which led to an ugly screaming match between him and us. I spent the next two weeks looking over my shoulder, convinced that he was coming for me and that I'd end up in the back of a cement mixer "by accident"!

Home Sweet Hell: Our first wreck, living up to its name.

TIPS FOR BUYING A WRECK

- Location is key. Everybody says this, and there is a reason why.

- Follow the creative community—young actors, artists, etc.—they are always the first to get into "up and coming" neighborhoods. We always try to buy in somewhat "fringe" areas as we know the deals are there. But you don't have to be the first ones: look for early signs of development, such as a great restaurant or boutique being built or a park being redone.

- The scarier the building looks, the better it is. A wreck intimidates most people, so you will always get a better price.

- Buy directly from the owner: it's easier and less expensive when you cut out the middleman.

- Get an engineer's report. If the structure is sound, you are golden. Get one contractor's bid before you buy and two more after.

- The space is your canvas; you can bring charm to any four walls.

THINGS TO CONSIDER BEFORE YOU RENOVATE

- Have a plan before you start. Imagine the worst-case scenario for every stage of the process and have a solution to fix it.

- Stylish spaces are great but if they don't function, it's a waste of time and money. Take time to think about how you use the various rooms in your house, and adapt your plans to suit that reality.

- Don't be too trendy—shag carpeting is still waiting for a comeback.

- Expensive doesn't always mean best.

One of the reasons we bought the property in Chelsea was the incredible view of the Empire State Building from the top floors. The historic landmark was built in a little over a year during the Depression in the 1930s. Remember that the next time your contractor tells you that it's going to take six months to redo your kitchen.

GET INSPIRED:
WHERE TO GO FOR IDEAS

At this point in the renovation, we had an empty shell, and while we had a vague idea of what we wanted to do, we still needed more inspiration. One of the things we learned during the process of building this house, which was underscored by the other houses we built later on, was that no matter what style you choose—traditional, contemporary, retro—you need to look at lots of examples of every kind of design scheme to know what works and doesn't work for you. We fuel our creativity by poring over hundreds of magazines and books. (If you don't want to spend money on buying them, set aside a weekend afternoon to spend in a bookshop with a café.)

Another important source for ideas is shops of all types. When we began to design our first house, more than ten years ago, it was hard to find or get access to sources and purveyors of great design that sold architectural artifacts, certain types of high-end products, and even various fabrics. We couldn't afford boutique furnishings in those early days, so it didn't matter all that much. But eventually we were able to splurge on certain items and wanted sources for them without having to resort to using a decorator—a lot of these items were available only to the trade, and you needed an interior decorator to purchase them for you. Fortunately, times have changed. Trade shows and design buildings are open to the public and the Internet has brought professional sourcing to anyone who is looking for it. With a little research, you can find just about anything.

INTERNET

You can Google anything. With eBay and countless design blogs that do a lot of the legwork finding amazing pieces, designing and decorating a house is easier than ever.

- Blogs we frequent are:

   Oh Happy Day (jordanferney.blogspot.com)

   Coco + Kelley (cocokelley.blogspot.com)

   Black*Eiffel (blackeiffel.blogspot.com)

   Decor 8 (decor8blog.com)

   Desire to Inspire
   (www.desiretoinspire.blogspot.com)

- Vacations: Go places that inspire and stimulate you. Hotels and retail stores have amazing design schemes— they are there for the taking! Carry a digital camera with you so you have a record of everything you see.

- Design trade shows: They are now open to the public, giving you the same access as professionals.

- Restaurants: They have amazing kitchens that have to be very functional. Ask the manager or owner where they got things—most are flattered to be asked.

- Big antique shows: For listings of ones in your area, look in the arts and design section of the newspaper.

MAGAZINES

Most magazines have detailed resource sections to purchase much of what you see in the magazine. We love:

- DOMINO
- ELLE DÉCOR
- METROPOLITAN HOME
- VOGUE LIVING

- LIVING, ETC. (UK)
- AUSTRALIAN VOGUE
- ELLE DECORATION (UK)
- DWELL

- SURFACE
- OBJEKT (NETHERLANDS)
- COOKIE

> "I have always
> imagined
> that Paradise
> will be a kind
> of library."
>
> —JORGE LUIS BORGES

We spend a lot of time looking at design books and magazines for ideas, and we've amassed a great library as a result. We generally buy any and every interior design book we see, and we particularly like getting books when we travel—a different perspective is key to creating interesting living spaces.

SHOPPING FOR A NEW HOUSE:
STYLE ON A SHOESTRING

FLEA MARKET CHIC

Here are some of the spoils we've scored at flea markets: the metal lights (far left) were used in one of our SoHo houses (pg. 60); the urn the kids are in is from a flea market in St. Tropez (middle bottom); and the low relief angel sculpture (above right) found its way to the facade of one the SoHo houses as well (pg. 51).

The house in Chelsea, just like our other early houses, was furnished and decorated with great flea market finds out of necessity—we found it was one of the easiest ways to bring charm to a house affordably. When we had a bit more money in our pocket years later, we realized we were still scouring flea markets and vintage shops because we loved what we saw: unique pieces that didn't look like they came out of a catalog.

BUYING VINTAGE FURNISHINGS ABROAD

When we were finally able to afford it, we loved going to flea markets in Europe. And buying and shipping antiques from other countries is much easier than one might imagine. The best way to begin is to strike up a relationship with a local dealer, as they will take you to places that you wouldn't have known existed otherwise. As with most situations in life, one person in the "know" can change your entire experience. The language barrier is something that we've never had much of a problem with; you'd be surprised how many people speak English when you are willing to buy their goods. Shipping is fairly easy as well. If you are only bringing one or two pieces home with you, bring two large duffle bags to fill for the flight home. If you are buying a lot, pay to get a container; you can also share one with someone else. Be sure to get shipping insurance. It's a good idea to write down everything that's in your shipment so that you remember what you bought.

HOW TO FLEA

- The great stuff sells before 6 AM; get there early, before the dealers snatch up the best things.

- Get a large cup of coffee—it's too early to be up on a weekend.

- Negotiate. You can always walk away and go back later.

- Be sure to bring the measurements of the spaces you are furnishing and a tape measure when shopping. A great table won't do you much good if you can't fit it through the front door.

- If you are in a foreign country, bring a pen and paper to write your price on just in case they don't understand you. Although I must admit that I have bought items all over the world speaking only English with a heavy Southern accent!

- While great merchandise is snapped up early, you can still get stuff at the end of the day—that is when the real bargains happen. No dealer wants to lug a giant armoire back onto his truck.

THE YELLOW TICKET: One of the highlights of our shopping sprees in Paris was working with the shipper Camard. They have been in business for four centuries and are located in the center of the Clignancourt. The way Camard works is that you tell them the amount of money that you think you'll spend and in turn they give you little yellow tickets and a notepad of receipts, which you use for purchases anywhere at the entire flea market or any antique store in Paris. After negotiating your price, you simply write down the dealer's address and give them a yellow ticket; later Camard picks it up, packages it, and has it shipped directly to you. Vive la France.

The perfect "flea market chic" bedroom. Much of what we used to decorate this room came from our local flea market, including the bed frame, the wicker bench at the foot of the bed, the ceiling lamp, and even some of the fabrics we used for the pillows.

THE INTERIOR

CREATING A WISH LIST

At the beginning of every project we create a wish list of the things that we really want and are willing to sacrifice others to make them happen. For this house, our wish list was:

- Brick wall between the kitchen and dining room.
- Stainless steel kitchen.
- Wood roof.
- Very high quality kitchen tile.
- One fantastic light fixture.

This old fireplace was one of the few original elements in the house we were able to save. Unfortunately, we did not have the $4,000 it would take to get it working. We got it fixed a few years later. You don't have to do everything at once.

We hired talented bricklayers to build
the arches—everyone thought they'd
been there for a hundred years.

This ornate mirror is beautifully worn and that's why we love it.

Dress up a plain bookcase or shelving unit by draping long strands of colorful beads across a corner. Just tack them on the top and back of the case with flat thumbtacks. We found this bookcase at a flea market and gave it a fresh coat of bright white paint.

DECORATING WITH FLEA MARKET FINDS

If you don't have a big budget for decorating your house, flea markets, garage sales, and vintage shops are the place to scour for bargains. With a little imagination, even the junkiest pieces can be brought back to life. This is just a sample of the rooms from this house, largely furnished on the cheap!

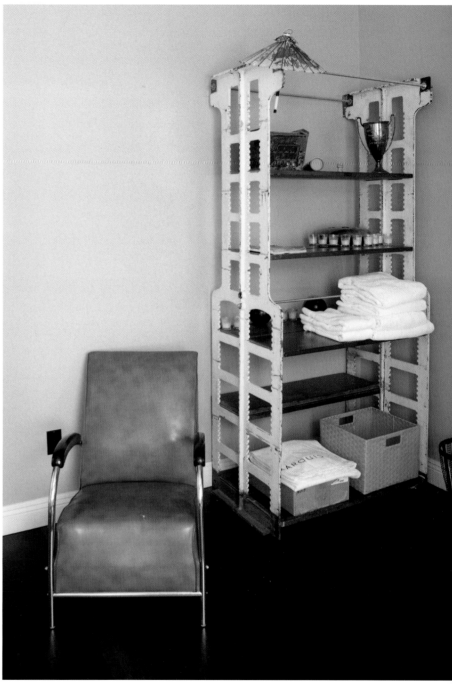

The chaise lounge was a hand-me-down from a relative. We put the zebra pillow on it to make it a bit more contemporary. It sits underneath a wall of posters, drawings, and paintings from flea markets hung salon style.

The library shelves in this bedroom were salvaged from Dartmouth University. We love to use furnishings with a past, a story. The chair, which worked perfectly with the blue color scheme, is a barber's chair. There was only one, which was fine by us. We don't feel like every chair needs a mate.

Robert was a huge fan of comic books as a kid, so when we found out that we were having our first child, we thought framing a bunch of old issues we found at a flea market in inexpensive frames would be a great way to decorate the baby's room.

For the Chelsea house, all of our money went into the structural work that needed to be done, which was considerable. This meant we were left with nearly no budget for furnishings. We borrowed many of our design concepts from ABC Home and Carpet, which was our favorite store at the time. We loved their paint schemes, lighting, fabrics, and decoration ideas—we just couldn't afford them. We bought old chairs and couches and had them reupholstered; found funky iron beds and painted them; stained and painted furniture; cut mirrors for table tops; and found fantastic vintage hardware for doorknobs and light fixtures. For curtains, we used a simple, cheap white fabric and had my girlfriend sew them—white usually looks good no matter what else is going on in a room.

We finally moved in two days before Thanksgiving. The house wasn't quite finished, so we put a tablecloth on the "gang box" (a large toolbox) and used it as a buffet. It was 35 degrees outside and the heat had not yet been turned on and my entire extended family was on their way from the South to spend the holiday with us. We called the electric company and they told us that it would be three weeks before they could get to us. I was three months pregnant and in a panic. There were a few guys from the electric company working on our street and I thought quickly. I went to the bakery, bought a huge box of cookies and a half dozen hot chocolates, and brought them to the workers. I gave them the best pregnant woman's plea that I could muster. We had heat that afternoon. Soon after, my family arrived and we had a great holiday.

"We spend all our time searching for security and hate it when we get it."

—JOHN STEINBECK

The "Wall of Women" in one of our guest rooms was made up of different pictures and paintings that I found at flea markets over the years. We loved the idea so much that we carried on the tradition of the all-girl theme for my daughters' room when they were born.

After they left, we finally finished the house. It had taken just under seven months to complete. We were elated but were also facing another challenge—we couldn't afford to live in it. We had three friends move into the third floor and Robert's sister moved into the garden apartment below.

Six months later Wolfgang (Wolfie) was born. Money was tight. In spite of the fact that we took on roommates, we still were not covering our expenses. We were two months behind on the mortgage and decided to rent out most of the house and move into the garden apartment. Within three months, we had cash in the bank for the first time. But before we had a chance to enjoy being in the black, the money was burning holes in our pockets and it was time for another project.

COLLECTIONS FOR THE WALL

A decorating trick we go back to time and time again is grouping similar objects on a wall, like the comic book wall (above left) and the wall of kitschy flea market images of women (above). Just remember that one element should be consistent among all the pieces of the collection: either size, color, or subject.

:: CHAPTER TWO

CHARMLESS TO CHARMING:

:: BEFORE

CASUAL CHIC IN THE CITY

WHAT WE DID

- Converted a 4,000-square-foot dreary commercial building into a single-family house.

- Gut renovated the entire house.

- Installed all new mechanicals (HVAC and plumbing).

- Built four "juliet" balconies.

- Added decorative grilles on all the windows.

- Refaced the facade with stucco.

- Built a foyer for privacy from the street.

- Incorporated vintage pieces throughout the house.

"Inside a ring or out, ain't nothing to do with going down. It's staying down that's wrong."

—MUHAMMAD ALI

AFTER

"A verbal contract isn't worth the paper it's written on."

—SAM GOLDWYN

THE FIRST STEPS

While we were living in Chelsea, we found an old commercial building that had absolutely no charm on the outskirts of SoHo on Thompson Street. It was undesirable for a few reasons: the main floor was at street level where people could look into the windows, and it was hideous. We got it for a great price, though, with the lot next door as part of the deal. The Soho Grand Hotel had just gone up, which was a sign that this part of the neighborhood was on the upswing.

The day after we closed, Robert went to meet with a contractor at the building to get a bid for his services. While he was waiting, another man approached him who said that he was doing construction at the Soho Grand. He somehow knew our building inside out. He set up an appointment with Robert to give us his own bid, which turned out to be half as much as everyone else's. We were incredibly stressed with financial problems and I was also pregnant with twins, so we stupidly hired him to do the demolition without knowing much about him. Within a week, we knew that we had made one of the worst mistakes of our lives. He turned out to be a crazy con man. Soon after, we fired him. Because of him, we were almost shut down and close to bankrupt. It was four months before he was out of our lives for good. But we moved on and soon hired another contractor and were ready to start anew.

HIRING YOUR CONTRACTOR

If your contractor looks like this guy, don't hire him.

CONTRACTOR CHECKLIST

:: Check references, check references, check references.

:: Inspect his recent work.

:: If all of his tools look new, be suspicious: he might be new to the trade.

:: Get everything in writing, even if you hire a friend or family member, which is never a good idea anyway.

:: Give very little money up front.

:: Get insurance certificates from the contractor and all of the sub-contractors, and make sure that you are on the policies.

:: Put a time completion clause in the contract.

PEOPLE YOU WANT ON YOUR TEAM

:: GENERAL CONTRACTOR: He is your eyes and ears and the most important person you hire. If you can't find one through word of mouth, find a local project that you like, find out who the contractor is, and ask for a card.

:: ENGINEER: The more prudent the better (your architect will provide you with an engineer).

:: SURVEYOR: Shows you precisely what your plot of land entails and where you can build.

:: EXPEDITOR: He can tell you the history of the property and what problems it may have had.

:: LAWYER: Have your lawyer review the terms of any and all contracts. We've had the same lawyer for eleven years. Find someone who takes your calls and acts as if you are his only client.

:: INSURANCE BROKER: The more insurance, the better.

"The crisis of today is the joke of tomorrow."

—H.G. WELLS

In the early phases of construction on this building we found ourselves getting frustrated and stressed easily and often. We had people dumping trash in our containers, a crazy neighbor who made false complaints to the city, our permits were getting torn down, and the building was getting covered with advertisements nightly. To put an end to the advertisements, our contractor painted a "post no bills" sign on the work site. The next day, someone spray painted pictures of Bill Murray all over the wall. We laughed for days. It was a great reminder not to take ourselves so seriously.

THE INTERIOR

THE CASUAL KITCHEN

As our style has evolved over the years, our kitchens have become a bit more modern. But we still love the more rustic kitchens of our early work like this one. A simple tall bookshelf served as a pantry and cupboard. This is certainly an inexpensive solution for storage but you need to be comfortable with the appearance—we didn't worry if everything wasn't well organized. The big wooden table and chairs were from a flea market—they were well worn, which we loved. The refrigerator was from a restaurant supply store.

Our biggest challenge with this project was to make the place charming. We invested in some architectural artifacts that would be the focal point of the building. Finding those artifacts was an adventure in itself. Despite the fact that I was pregnant with twins, I often found myself digging through attics in old farmhouses, or fifty stories up on top of scaffolding looking at artifacts on facades, or crawling through the ruins of demolished buildings hunting for flooring and tiles.

We decided to give the building a European look and feel by using stucco on the facade, and installing old shutters and a set of monastery gates that I found in Western Pennsylvania. We designed the ground floor to look like a French café. Because we lived quite casually, we turned the main floor into a large living space, a trend we've continued in all of our houses. We kept the space open and multifunctional. We painted the walls with orange Venetian plaster, which was incredibly striking. We used vintage lighting and doors throughout the house, adding charm where it didn't exist. During this project, we began to explore different looks and our style was beginning to evolve.

"No architecture can **be truly noble** that's not imperfect."

—JOHN RUSKIN

A week after we moved in, the house flooded, bowing the new hardwood floors. We didn't fix them because they "aged" the house in a really interesting way.

Because the house had plenty of light, we could experiment with darker, more interesting finishes for the walls. We wanted a silvery, glimmering effect which we created by mixing black artist paint with white plaster. We found the doors at our favorite architectural artifact store in New York, Olde Good Things. The desk was made from old industrial cabinets and a wood slab that we cut to fit.

THIS IS OUR CREDO:
:: Experiment :: Take risks :: Have fun :: Explore
:: Change :: Invent :: Change again

A photo wall is a great way of showing off your family tree. Our kids look at it all the time and love to hear stories about the relatives in the pictures.

TURNING NEGATIVES INTO POSITIVES

:: We placed flower boxes In front of each window, giving us a bit more privacy.

:: We covered the ugly fake brick facade with stucco, which gave the building a beautiful finish.

:: After a terrible flood, we raised the doorway to eliminate water problems.

:: We soundproofed all of the bedroom windows, dampening the noise from the street.

:: We found gorgeous tile for the front steps, but there wasn't enough. We mixed it with cement, which gave it a vintage look (right).

:: The bathroom off one of the guest bedrooms couldn't accommodate a door so we improvised one with a beaded curtain (opposite top).

:: Some of the bedrooms had lots of light but the hallways that adjoined them were dark, so we installed glass doors to make sure the light reached the core of the house (opposite bottom).

"You must lose a fly to catch a trout."

—GEORGE HERBERT

Music, flowers, candles, and some good
wine make for a great party. Your home is
not a museum—enjoy it.

WE'RE FINISHED:
TIME TO CELEBRATE

No matter what style we are attempting
to achieve in a house, our first priority
is to make it a place where people feel
comfortable. We love to entertain: it doesn't
matter if it's for twenty kids or 150 of our
friends—our home should be a place where
people want to hang out and not be afraid to
spill a drink or take off their shoes.

After spending two of three years
pregnant, Robert and I were ready to throw
a lot of parties when we moved into the
Thompson Street house. We found lots
of reasons to celebrate: a house warming,
holidays, birthdays, an art opening, and the
girls' christening. We've had all of our kids
baptized in the living room, which might not
be completely legitimate in the church's eyes,
but it works for us. The celebrations were
beautiful and there was always a fantastic
reception afterward.

Of course, we didn't always wait until a
house was finished to have a good time in it.
Our next project was in front of us, and once
the shell of the house was constructed, we
decided to throw a party in it (see next page).
The point is: don't wait until your house is
perfectly decorated, or spotless, or whatever
other reason you can come up with for not
enjoying family and friends in your home.

We found these old table numbers in Paris, and we
use them for decoration now. It's the unique touches,
and often small ones, that people remember.

> "Music produces a
> kind of pleasure
> which human nature
> cannot do without."
>
> —CONFUCIUS

Fillers* are Fun: With as many kids as
we have, it's tough to see our friends as
often as we'd like, so we throw a few big
parties every year and invite everyone
we know. Unfortunately, as a lot of
people get older, they take themselves a
little too seriously and/or get extremely
dull. Therefore, we rely often on "fillers"
to add new life to the festivities. We
threw this catered party in a space that
we had just begun construction on.

*Random person or newfound friend who is
usually younger, more fun, and interesting than
those in your current social circle.

KIDS' PARTIES

:: Four-year-olds don't need RSVPs.

:: Kids are there to celebrate their friend's birthday, not to receive extravagant goody bags.

:: We always serve beer and wine to the adults, but never to the kids.

:: Never get your face too close to the stick when it's time for the piñata.

Parties should be fun and shouldn't be stressful. Recently, an over-anxious mom asked me how I throw so many birthday parties for my children. I told her, "I bake a cake and invite a bunch of kids." Sometimes—most times—it's that simple.

:: CHAPTER THREE

PARIS MEETS GOTHAM:

FRENCH URBAN FLAIR

:: BEFORE

WHAT WE DID

:: Built a 75-foot-tall home on a 20-x-50-foot lot, from the ground up.

:: Installed pylons 100 feet deep.

:: Installed all mechanicals (HVAC and plumbing).

:: Built a garage and installed an elevator.

:: Attached fluted pilasters to the front facade to frame the front door and garage.

:: Built the home with artifacts from all over the world.

:: Added vintage balconies from Peru on the front and back facades.

:: Installed resalvaged tile from a cathedral on the kitchen floor.

:: Salvaged a low relief angel sculpture from a hotel going out of business and placed it on the facade.

"Once you sink that first stake, they'll never make you pull it up."

– ROBERT MOSES

If you told me that I would design the tallest house in downtown Manhattan when I was struggling with math in high school, I never would have believed you.

AFTER

THE FIRST STEPS

Our next project was awaiting us and we didn't have to go far—it was the vacant lot next door to the Thompson Street house we had just completed. Before we could start building, we had to have the commercial lot rezoned for residential use. In order to do that, Robert and I had to gather 150 signatures in forty-eight hours. Somehow, we did it; and five months and three community board meetings later, we had the zoning. We were overjoyed. The lot, which came free with the purchase of the house next door, was now worth a substantial amount of money.

Before we could build, we had to install sixteen 100-foot pylons into our tiny lot, which was surrounded by three buildings. Putting these giant pylons in causes intense vibrations, often resulting in foundational damage to the surrounding buildings. We were petrified and instructed by our prudent engineer to pay double the cost for the hydraulic type which didn't cause as much vibration. They were an enormous expense but in the end, it was a wise decision to use them. After the "piles" were installed, they had to be tested, and testing day fell on the most hectic weekend of our lives. That Friday, Robert resigned from his brokerage firm of eight years. Saturday was the pylon test. Our entire street had to be shut down in order to do the archaic test, which involved lowering two 5000-pound blocks of cement onto the piles from an 80-foot-tall crane. If we didn't pass, we'd have to redo them and it would cost $150,000—money we didn't have. And on Sunday, I brought Breaker, our fourth child, home from the hospital. Robert was with me, but an hour earlier he'd just finished running the New York Marathon. We didn't know if we were coming or going, but we passed the test and were blessed with another healthy baby.

Once the structural work was done we were ready for the fun part. We went to Paris to shop for artifacts to build into the house. For six wonderful days Robert, his parents, and I shopped and filled a container with over two hundred antiques and artifacts. We found incredible pieces, including two large circular windows that came from an old cathedral. We bought them, knowing that we'd have to change all of the blueprints for the building. Sixty days later the container arrived in New York, full of windows, lighting, tiles, fabric, hardware, and furniture. It felt like Christmas. Everything that we unpacked was in perfect condition. Vive la France, again.

THE INTERIOR

We were going for a French industrial look in the living room. We painted the floors black and added new doors and painted them black as well. We installed new tin ceilings and painted them gold. We left the sprinklers exposed and added vintage lights that we found in Paris. We mixed an old post with a new staircase, and salvaged an old mirror from the Biltmore Hotel.

Every time we took someone on a tour of the house, we explained to them that we built it from the ground up. Without fail, by the time they got to the fourth floor, they asked us what year it was built.

The last day of construction proved to be one of the most dramatic when our head carpenter took two sips of turpentine thinking it was Diet Coke. We can laugh at it now because after two days in the hospital, he recovered. But we still can't figure out why he took that second sip.

It seemed luck was on our side on several fronts as we rented out the original Thompson Street house and moved into the new one, which we were certain we'd spend the next twenty years in.

"The reality of the building does not consist of the roof and walls, but in the space within to be lived in."
—LAO TZU

I read recently in a magazine that a designer was really proud that a house he designed looked just like a famous showroom. I am not sure that is a good thing. Your space should actually look like people live there.

An old bar base we bought in Paris was brought back to life with a new zinc countertop, which is also from Paris.

OLD GOOD THINGS

- Using vintage pieces in new spaces is very distinctive.

- Any door can be refinished to its original look, including the locks and doorknobs.

- Great old light fixtures can be rewired to today's codes.

- Old tile can be mixed with new tile.

- New glass can make old windows functional.

"It is better to **fail in originality** than to **succeed in imitation.**"

— BEN FRANKLIN

Our brand new kitchen had the look of an old loft. We exposed the sprinkler to replicate the old look. The clock was purchased in Paris and we had it fixed locally.

"It takes a lot of courage to show your dreams to someone else."

—ERMA BOMBECK

VINTAGE ARTIFACTS:
THE AGONY AND THE ECSTASY

There is no doubt that furnishing and decorating a house with vintage pieces can be slightly more difficult than just going to your favorite furniture store and selecting an entire room straight from the sales floor. If you don't have the energy for a whole house of vintage pieces, just add one or two in your favorite room.

We use antique plumbing fixtures in our projects, like this unique double sink (opposite), and we are happy to put up with the variety of quirks that come along with using vintage pieces. But if you can't find one, or don't want to hassle with vintage plumbing, look at the products that companies like Kohler make, which can have a vintage feel. They tend be more affordable and function well.

We found the amazing cornice (above) at a flea market and just nailed it to the top of the window frame. It set the tone for the vintage elements in the room, like the antique pendant lamps, the plaster decorative reliefs next to the window, and the blank ornate frames on the wicker storage container.

I inherited this chair from my grandmother. To make it more our style, we had it reupholstered in a zebra-pattern fabric. Mixing different styles—old-fashioned furniture with cool, contemporary fabrics—is one of the keys to bringing a unique flavor to a house.

We found these old factory lights in Paris and paid $100 for all of them. After rewiring them to U.S. code, they were as good as new.

CREATING A FOCAL POINT

One of riskiest things we did to this house was installing the cathedral rose window, but it was a risk that paid off. When you have a focal point like this in a room—such as a dramatic oversized mirror, a dazzling chandelier, or great piece of art—everything else in the room can be a bit more plain so as not to distract from the visual punch that the piece gives a room.

We found this cathedral window in Paris, after our building plans had already been approved. It was so magnificent that we knew we had to make it a part of this house. To bring a piece of Paris to New York City was something special. Thank goodness the dimensions of the window worked. When working with a contractor or an architect, make sure that they are flexible and will make changes that won't be prohibitively expensive.

"An architect's most useful tools are an erasure at the drafting board and a wrecking bar at the site."

—FRANK LLOYD WRIGHT

:: CHAPTER FOUR

HOME AWAY FROM HOME

:: BEFORE

THE COOL COUNTRY HOUSE

WHAT WE DID

:: Gut renovated a one-hundred-year-old farmhouse in Great Barrington, Massachusetts.

:: Opened up the ground floor, turning a lot of small rooms into a big loftlike space.

:: Installed all new mechanicals (HVAC and plumbing).

:: Transformed the attic into a playroom.

:: Built a fence around the property, for safety and privacy.

:: Added a pool, spa, and deck.

:: Replaced old glass in doors with cheap Plexiglas, which has a mod look.

:: Installed an in-ground trampoline.

:: Added a new wood burning fireplace that heats the house, cutting down on energy costs during the winter.

:: Installed inexpensive, simple shades paired with new, high quality hardware on the windows.

"What's a joy to the one
is a nightmare to the other."

—BERTOLT BRECHT

THE FIRST STEPS

The house looked and smelled like a musty
hunting lodge. It had several small rooms,
each of which had five or six layers of
wallpaper on the walls. And that was the
good news. Some of the other rooms were
covered in wood paneling, the carpets were
soiled, smelly and rotted, and the heat didn't
work. By simply knocking down the interior
walls, pulling up the carpet, and throwing
out the old appliances and cabinetry, the
house was transformed within a week. But
we still had a lot of work ahead of us and it
was still really cold.

   We brought our workers from the city
to do all of the construction, except for the
electric and plumbing, for which we hired
local guys. We realized that the place was
not perfect and didn't try to make it so—we
fixed what we could. The wood floors were
dark and old, so we painted them white,
which immediately brightened up the whole
place. We kept the doors but replaced the
old glass with inexpensive Plexiglas, giving
them a mod look. We bought inexpensive
cabinets at Home Depot and transformed
them with great hardware.

   This house has been good to us. Not
only has it been a great place for the kids to
escape city life and develop an appreciation
of nature, but it's also been a terrific
investment. Before we purchased it, we
were paying $1,500 a month for storage in
New York. We buy things for new projects
all the time and have always needed ample
space to store them until we are ready to use
them. The house has a large garage with a
guesthouse above it (more storage) and our
mortgage is less than half what we were
paying for storage in New York.

:: AFTER

THE INTERIOR

Rural New England was a welcome change from the hustle and bustle of New York City. Robert and I grew up in the suburbs, so we never had any extended time in more pastoral parts of the South where we grew up. We were happy we could offer our kids a taste of the country. Here are some tips if you decide a house in the country is for you:

:: Have respect for the local people—it's their town.

:: Let the home become an investment. We rent ours for the month of August and for some weekends in the winter to help pay the mortgage.

:: It's a good idea to have a neighbor check on your house when you aren't there, so be sure to befriend one (or more)!

:: You can swap places with people from all over the world or lend it to friends.

:: Remember not to put too much money into the house and avoid the scene at left: endless bills and headaches from an overly ambitious renovation project. Otherwise, you could price yourself out of the real value.

"We believe that electricity exists because the electric company keeps sending us bills for it, but we cannot figure out how it travels inside."

—DAVE BARRY

This is what we were waiting for: after all the construction, we had the clean, bright space we wanted. We painted the floors and walls white on the first floor, and just added pops of color, like in the chair, pillows, and tall vase here. We think playful décor lightens the mood in any house, so we particularly like this oversized flower pot sculpture.

THE MINIMAL KITCHEN

Simplicity was essential for the kitchen in this house. We wanted clean lines and neutral colors for the tables and cabinets. The table, cabinets, and center island were all made of white laminate. We like stainless steel refrigerators and this one fit perfectly into our pared down aesthetic. To make sure the overall effect wasn't too severe, we hung colorful art and added chairs for the kitchen table in different colors.

Design is not making beauty. Beauty emerges from selection, affinities, integration, love."

—LOUIS KAHN

The kitchen is where we spend a lot of our time so we didn't want it to seem like an afterthought in terms of the furnishings and décor. We installed inexpensive cabinets but replaced the hardware with sleek door pulls and knobs, which made them far more interesting. In the dining room, a set of groovy chairs spruced up a simple, inexpensive table. And we mixed contemporary art and antiques throughout the house.

"People think the Beatles
know what's going on.
We don't. We're just doing it."

—JOHN LENNON

CHEAP CHIC:

HOW LOW CAN YOU GO?

:: Brown folding chairs: $50

:: Blue leather chairs: $250 each

:: Cappelini table (floor model, 40% off)

:: Faux snakeskin dining chairs: $80 each

:: Kartell "Ghost" plastic chair: $100 at a
   close out sale

:: Walter Niedermayer photographs:
   priceless!

SUNROOMS

The essential element of any sunroom is a cozy nook or comfy couch for long naps. For ours, we used a vintage daybed covered with inexpensive throw pillows and a faux fur bedspread. We also have a generously stuffed easy chair, perfect for reading a book on a sunny afternoon.

"The details are not details. They make the design."

—CHARLES EAMES

This beautiful sunroom doubles as our office in the country. It's where we keep our computers, files, and design books. Organizing a work space in your vacation home gives you more reasons to stay longer.

"Art resides in the quality of doing,
process is not magic."

—CHARLES EAMES

We love staying at the house in the winter. There are great ski slopes just three miles away, and fortunately all the kids have learned to ski. A season's ski pass for the family costs $150, which is great since we have six kids.

DETAILS, DETAILS, DETAILS

Books, like anything else in a house, can add a decorative flourish. In our family room, we added pops of color with a red and a blue book for the coffee table.

While we kept the walls and floors on the ground floor white, we used a lot more color upstairs. The kids' rooms in particular are done with really happy, vibrant colors.

"Red is the ultimate cure for sadness."

—BILL BLASS

BE BOLD:
USE COLOR

All the bedrooms in this country house, from the master to the kids' rooms, are painted with bright, bold colors. When we do this, we try to keep everything else in the room (except the art) relatively neutral—lots of white for bedding and furniture.

"The colors I use may clash or vibrate against each other but that's done intentionally."

—FRANK BRUNO

"It is the eye of ignorance that assigns a fixed and unchangeable color to every object. Beware of this stumbling block."

—PAUL GAUGUIN

OUTDOOR SPACES

"Almost every time I make a building,
some people will condemn it straight to Hell."

—ARNE JACOBSEN

THE YELLOW SHUTTERS: While we were painting the house, we decided that we wanted a mod color for the shutters, something different from all of the black and dark green that we saw all over New England. Once they were painted, we found out that the locals referred to our house as the one with "those yellow shutters."

Soon after, our eight-year-old was being driven home from a play date. As they approached the house, the friend said, "My mom thinks that you have the ugliest shutters in Massachusetts." Our son came home and asked us to please, please paint them another color. We haven't—we still like the yellow.

DECORATING THE OUTSIDE OF YOUR HOUSE

You can dress up the exterior of a house the same way you can the interior. The yellow striped curtains that hang in the portico (left) were made from durable outdoor umbrella fabric. We simply cut the fabric to fit, sewed the edges, and bolted the fabric to the top wooden beam. The peace sign made of twine (right) was yet another simple but powerful element on the side of our house. We asked a local florist to make it for us, and it wasn't much more expensive than a large Christmas wreath—and it lasts a lot longer!

"Anybody can be good in the country, there are no temptations there."

—OSCAR WILDE

POOL ADVICE

:: Pools are expensive; don't put one in unless you are going to use it a lot.

:: Many realtors will tell you that pools do not add value to your home; your kids will not agree.

:: Grass is cheaper than deck or tile, and tile is hot on the feet.

:: Heated pools are great— especially if you have wimpy city kids.

:: Instead of a predictable diving board for the pool, we built a wooden platform, because it reminded us of a dock over a lake. And because it's bigger, all the kids can stand on it at the same time.

We bought our country hous because we fell in love with th land. It was worth more than th price of the house. It's easy t renovate a home but it takes a lon time to get greenery like this

"Simplicity is the ultimate sophistication."

—LEONARDO DA VINCI

GREAT TOYS:
TRAMPOLINES

One addition to the country house that has provided endless hours of entertainment for our kids is the trampoline in the backyard. We sunk it into the ground so it would be safer and not too conspicuous on the lawn. To do this we:

:: Dug a hole approximately 3 feet deep (the height of the trampoline).

:: Used wood 2 x 4s to build the foundation.

:: Built a simple drainage system.

:: Laid rocks for irrigation.

"Think sideways."

—EDWARD DE BONO

Why does every neighborhood in America have the same family, the one with a big blue trampoline and eight nonworking cars in the front yard?

:: CHAPTER FIVE

FUN HOUSE

:: BEFORE

A PLACE FOR ENTERTAINING

WHAT WE DID

- Knocked down the entire building, except for the party walls (side walls).

- Installed all new mechanicals (HVAC and plumbing).

- Built four separate outdoor spaces.

- Installed balconies on the front facade.

- Built a custom bar, game room, and wine cellar.

- Installed wenge floors (expensive dark wood from Africa).

- Installed a spalike bathroom, including a steam shower.

- Installed a showroom model of a designer kitchen purchased at 50% off list price.

- Built an intercom and stereo system that was wired throughout the house.

"Don't buy the house.

:: AFTER

Buy the neighborhood."

—RUSSIAN PROVERB

FIRST STEPS

After a year of searching the streets of downtown Manhattan for a new property, Robert and I came across a block that we never knew existed, called Centre Market Place. It's a tiny block in SoHo tucked right behind the historic police building, a grand domed structure. When we found it, there were four dilapidated gun shops in various states of ruin that were all for sale. When we learned that the gun shops could be converted into single-family homes, we knew that this was our dream project—and certainly the largest one that we had ever undertaken. We weren't just transforming a single house, but the character of nearly an entire street. We took every cent we had and mortgaged our entire future, knowing that what we were about to do was going to be fantastic. We were able to presell 4 Centre Market Place to a client that had been interested in one of our other properties, which financed the project and minimized our risk. We then sold the other two buildings, also preconstruction through an ad in the *New York Times*, which saved us a fortune in broker fees. We kept the fourth property for ourselves.

The client who purchased 4 Centre Market was a fun-loving single guy who asked us to build him the ultimate bachelor pad. He was not the type of person who wanted to go to paint stores or look through shelter magazines, so the two of us ran around the city looking at boutique hotels, cool restaurants, and clubs for fun design ideas. We had a great time doing it, although it was tiring because I was pregnant with our second set of twins. Once we figured out what he wanted, he gave us the complete freedom to build and design a house where he could entertain four hundred of his closest friends.

Centre Market Place, circa 1930s.

Centre Market Place, today. So many of the old-time residents on Centre Market Place have complimented us by saying how nice it is to see kids playing on the street for the first time in thirty years.

"I can live for two months on a good compliment."

—MARK TWAIN

For this house, we approached the kitchen and living areas as we had before—one big open space. Again, this is for people who want to live a bit more casually, so it's certainly not ideal for everyone. But we find our clients are more and more interested in configuring their spaces like this, regardless of where they live or how big their house is. Even though many of our clients don't cook, they still insist on having big,

beautiful kitchens. (As most people know, a great kitchen helps with the resale value.) For this lemon yellow and stainless steel kitchen, we were on a relatively strict budget. So we did what we do often for our projects: we bought the floor model right off the sales floor for 50% off the list price. To do the same for your house, be sure to visit your local kitchen showrooms often and ask about similar opportunities.

"Luxury must be comfortable, otherwise it's not luxury."

—COCO CHANEL

THE "COOK'S" KITCHEN

This client was not a big cook, but he did plan to entertain a lot so he wanted a fully stocked kitchen with all the bells and whistles: two large ovens, every kind of high-end appliance available, a huge stainless steel island that has a recessed gas cooktop, and of course, a Sub-Zero refrigerator. When Robert was younger, he worked for a family that had an industrial kitchen, and when we finally installed a Sub-Zero in our own kitchen, as well as in our client's, he felt like he had finally "made it."

"Happiness is not a station to arrive at,
but a manner of traveling."
—MARGARET LEE RUNBECK

All of the antiques in this wine cellar came from our house. We usually end up selling many of our best pieces to clients or dealers, and sometimes we trade with stores or they put pieces on consignment. Mixing great vintage pieces with new or modern spaces brings a sense of warmth and history to a room.

THE GLOBAL ROOM:

In addition to pairing vintage and new furnishings, we're always using stuff we love from all over the world. This room is a great example of that: the blue column is from India; the desk came from a science lab in Paris; the globe came from Belgium; we found the lights in South Carolina; the wastebasket is French; and the blue chair is from the Downtown Athletic Club in Manhattan.

DETAILS, DETAILS, DETAILS

The element that makes this bathroom (opposite) unique is the Tissus Coton sign, a great find in a local flea market. Paired with bright green walls, the otherwise streamlined and neutral bathroom is very dramatic. Sometimes all you need is one great piece to make a room stand out.

GAME ROOMS

Pinball machines and video games are great additions to any game room. They can be expensive but it's still possible to find them at reasonable prices. We bought ours on eBay, but a word to the wise: make sure they are in mint condition. They are not easily moved or repaired, so you want one that will last a while.

We bought the table, the yellow chair, the lamp, and the rug in Nice, France, at the flea market. None of these items cost more than $300. The shots of Tupac and Easy E were taken by Chi Modu.

A requisite part of any bachelor pad is a game room. For this one, the palette is dark, which is more masculine, but then we added pops of color to make the room a bit more fun.

The wenge floors were very expensive but the client insisted. We were able to cut costs in other parts of the house to accommodate them. The pool table was a fabulous find at an antiques show. The owner was specific about the look he wanted for the walls and we were able to achieve it by mixing black paint with plaster (which we had done in one of the Thompson Street houses). The somewhat chalky effect of the walls was contrasted by the high-gloss, bright white paint for the ceiling. The Art Deco–inspired pool table looks great with the 1950s Deco lights from Paris. And the stainless steel and glass door was salvaged from a YMCA.

"The home should be the treasure chest of living."

—LE CORBUSIER

HOME BARS

If you see a bar that you love, take pictures. We saw one similar to this, fell in love with it, and returned a few days later with a carpenter. He did his drawings right there at the bar. But if bringing your carpenter to the bar you want to copy is not an option, remember that a master carpenter can replicate anything simply by looking at a picture. If you need more information, ask the bartender—they are known to talk a lot and are usually fonts of information. We topped this bar with a zinc counter that was fabricated in Paris.

"Give me the
luxuries of life
and I will willingly do
without the necessities."

—FRANK LLOYD WRIGHT

When we were designing the bachelor's house we were moving toward a more contemporary look. He let us mix modern pieces with French antiques. One bit of consistent positive feedback we get on our work is our ability to create a brand new room that has the patina of history. To get that look in this room, we used vintage tin ceilings, an antique mirror, and old Moroccan tiles to give the new construction an old "personality."

"The secret to business is to know something that no one else knows."

—ARISTOTLE ONASSIS

WE'RE FINISHED:
TIME TO START OUR COMPANY

When we were done building the bachelor pad, we had another extraordinary project under our belts and we were ready, finally, to make building and designing houses our full-time jobs. Our dreams were all coming true—we founded our own company, Sixx Design. After all of the moving around and buying and selling of houses, we finally had the financial freedom to live our passion and to wake up every morning excited to work, loving what we do. We were preparing to build three more houses on Centre Market Place, including one for ourselves, a home we'd been fantasizing about for over a decade.

We named our company Sixx Design because of our six kids. It seems so obvious now to say this but it helped us immensely to formalize what we were doing by creating a business. We were no longer just Robert and Cortney, and people began to take us more seriously.

"They are happy men whose natures sort with their vocations."

—FRANCIS BACON

:: CHAPTER SIX

FULL HOUSE:
SIX KIDS, TWO SETS OF TWINS, AND US

:: BEFORE

WHAT WE DID

:: Demolished everything except for the party walls.

:: Repositioned ceiling beams to raise the height to 11 feet.

:: Installed all new mechanicals (HVAC and plumbing).

:: Built a basketball court on the roof.

:: Installed a steel staircase that was fabricated in Belgium.

:: Installed mahogany doors and window frames off steel baseboards.

:: Fabricated and installed glass balconies, attached to the building with steel plates.

:: Built a theater in the basement.

:: Installed a retractable glass garage door between the back patio and kitchen.

:: Installed a working vintage fountain on the back wall of the outdoor patio.

:: Used white Venetian plaster on walls throughout.

" Each new situation requires a new architecture."

—JEAN NOUVEL

THE FIRST STEPS

:: AFTER

After ten years of building and selling houses, not to mention moving countless times, we were finally in the position to build the house that we had always wanted. Our plan was to live in it forever (hopefully). We knew exactly what we wanted and had every detail planned—from the light switches to the air vents to the glass balconies. We took everything to a new level: a basketball court on the roof, stainless steel stair railings, white plaster walls, mahogany doors, a home theater, and our art collection. We had fallen in love with modern design and wanted to build a house that had clean lines and a sleek contemporary look yet had the warmth of a home, not an office building. We had six kids after all—we didn't want to live in a museum. So, we mixed stainless steel and glass with materials with interesting textures, soft fabrics, and gorgeous woods. We used white Venetian plaster for the walls which was complemented by the mahogany doors and white oak floors. This warmed up the stainless steel throughout the house. We also added vintage lighting.

As we had in most of our projects, we combined vintage with contemporary, from hanging an old chandelier over a modern soap stone tub to arranging antique leather chairs around a new white lacquer table.

"Don't compromise yourself.

You're all you've got."

—JANIS JOPLIN

One Sunday afternoon, Robert and I were eating at Felix, a French restaurant in our neighborhood and our favorite place to have brunch. There was a table next to us of six or seven people and two of the women were wearing the exact same yellow dress. There was another table close by of people who seemed to be having a very good time, and they soon noticed the matching frocks and started chanting "same dress, same dress, same dress." The entire placed joined in. It was very funny, although neither of the women looked like they thought so.

The point is: do you really want your home to look like everyone else's?

"Good architecture lets nature in.

—MARIO PEI

THE INTERIOR

The kitchen and living area is where we spend most of our time at home. As always, we made it a big open space but this time we also installed a retracting glass garage door between the kitchen and patio, bringing the outside inside. It's wonderful when the weather is nice and we can leave it open. The fountain in the back is two hundred years old and was salvaged from France.

One of the questions we are most often asked is how we maintain a thriving, and exhausting, business and run after six kids between the ages of three and eleven. The answer is: it's not easy. But with planning, patience, and a good dose of practicality, we make it work. We don't obsess over silly things like making sure we have a home-cooked meal every night, as my favorite recipe below attests to:

Homemade Dish by Cortney Novogratz

Serves: 4 to 6
Time: 35 to 45 minutes, depending on how long it takes you to flip through the phone book

INGREDIENTS
• Telephone
• Phone Book
• Cash or Credit Card
• Favorite Cocktail

Flip through the phone book. Find the number of your favorite restaurant that delivers. Place phone in hand, and dial the number. Order 4 to 6 of their tastiest dishes. Add 2 to 3 desserts to your order. (Optional.) Pour your favorite cocktail, lounge back with your feet up, and wait 30 to 40 minutes. Dish is done when your doorbell rings. Leftovers can be held in the fridge for one to two days.

"We have to start teaching ourselves

not to be afraid."

—WILLIAM FAULKNER

BE BOLD:
USE COLOR

As you might have guessed from looking at our other projects, we love orange and we've used it in virtually all of our houses. It's very modern, but when it's used with more traditional fabrics, like the damask curtains and pillows here, it's very luxurious.

When we first started out, we made simple curtains with inexpensive fabrics to save money. As our budget increased, we were able to order custom curtains with heavier fabrics. Ultimately, heavier fabrics are more durable and with lots of kids who aren't as careful as I would like sometimes, they wear better. I like to add color to a space with furnishings and accessories, and curtains are great place to be a bit bolder with color, like this deep saffron.

"Take your shoes off. Y'all come back now, y'hear."

—JED CLAMPETT

Six kids means a lot of friends and a constant stream of play dates. We have days when there are easily eight or ten kids running through the house. I always tell the kids who come over that they can take their shoes off or leave them on—just make sure not to forget them when they leave.

"Enthusiasm is life."

—PAUL SCOFIELD

MIXING HIGH AND LOW

We consistently mix furnishings and decorative elements from all prices levels. Our bedroom is a great example of this:

HIGH

:: Goose feather lamp from Moss.

:: Oil painting above our bed by Brendan Cass.

:: Matching fabric for the curtains and bed frame.

LOW

:: $25 nightstand from a garage sale that I painted white.

:: Kitschy statuette and long-necked vase were just dollars a piece at a flea market.

:: Throw pillows are from Target.

We rarely have headboards for our beds; this saves money, makes for a more streamlined look, and allows us to hang art over the beds.

"I collect antiques. Why? Because they're beautiful." —BRODERICK CRAWFORD

BATHROOMS

I think it's very important to personalize a bathroom. In mine,
I have mini statues of goddesses and cupids on both the counter
for the sink and the storage unit behind the tub. And these can be
functional, too: I hang bracelets and necklaces on the large one
next to my sink (see opposite). The nonelectric chandelier above
the tub was my idea as well. Instead of lights (it's illegal to put a lamp
or anything electric over a tub for obvious reasons), I put candles in
the sockets when I take a bath. The whole room sparkles.

I love collecting keepsakes from all over the world. But the
world is becoming so homogenized that even SoHo, our wonderful
neighborhood, is starting to look like a strip mall. All of the great
cities are beginning to resemble each other. Last year, we flew to
São Paulo, and one of the first things we saw when we got off the
plane and stepped into the airport was a Gap. Argghh. Be sure
to support the unique boutiques and shops in your town or they
won't last much longer.

For years I have been collecting the perfume bottles shown here
from each place that we visit. I think that they look great mixed in
with a few pieces of kids' art.

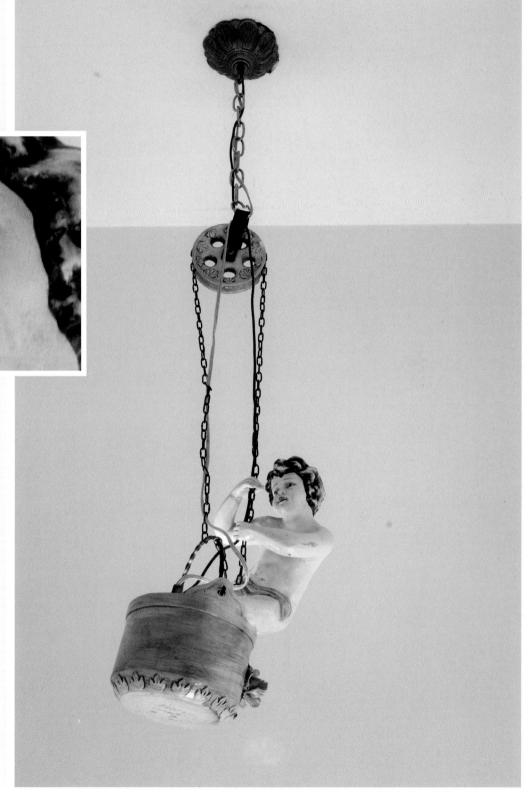

UNIQUE LIGHTING

Using vintage lighting has become one of the signature elements of our work. We have always been obsessed with light fixtures. And it's surprisingly easy to rewire vintage lights, or even hardware that was never intended to be a light. The blue police light (opposite top left) was given to us by the precinct across the street—it's always good to be friends with cops! The dazzling multibulb light (opposite top right), which we used in our kitchen, is from an old hotel in Monte Carlo. The star-shaped lights (opposite bottom) we used in one of our earliest houses was a flea market find, as was the quirky lady light (right) we found in Chelsea for $100.

...simply means you can't repair it yourself."

—FRANK CAPRA

HOME THEATERS:
WHAT WE'VE LEARNED

- :: If you are creating a new space that will need electronics, buy them after everything else is finished, as prices come down monthly.

- :: Keep it simple; never buy anything that requires nine remotes and opt for as few speakers, wires, and gadgets as possible.

- :: We tried to make the home theater as multifunctional as possible, as it doubles as the kids' playroom.

- :: Movie theater seats are not all that comfortable—use big chairs and couches.

- :: If you are installing a projector, make sure that you do it in a room that can be completely dark.

- :: Don't believe the philosophy that the most expensive and latest gadgets are best—go for the most reliable.

With six kids, we wanted to create a space where they could have the freedom to be kids, but we wanted the style to reflect us so it fits into the aesthetic of the rest of the house. We turned the basement into a playroom by day and home theater by night. We added lots of storage for the kids' toys and kept the space open enough for them to play. The furnishings are modern but cozy enough for movie watching. The floors are polished cement, which have a nice clean look and they are indestructible.

OUTDOOR SPACES

ROOF DECKS

A perfect roof is incredibly important. I can't tell you enough how many times we have patched or fixed a roof only to have it leak again. **DO IT RIGHT THE FIRST TIME.** Make sure it is a burned membrane roof and the water is pitched to the drains. In addition, get a thirty-year guarantee (in writing) from the roofer, and, always check references.

After we spent so much money on the deck, we wanted to make sure our views weren't obstructed so we installed glass railings.

The speed of change
makes you wonder what will become
of architecture."

—TADAO ANDO

"All architecture is shelter,

all great architecture is the design of space that contains, cuddles, exalts, or stimulates the persons in that space."

—PHILIP JOHNSON

Building a basketball court on the roof was one of the most exciting projects that we have undertaken. We designed the dome over the court to mirror the dome of the police building across the street. We asked the guy who built our stairs to fabricate the dome in stainless steel and complimented it with a synthetic wire mesh that we discovered in the back of a magazine.

:: CHAPTER SEVEN

THE DREAM HOUSE ABROAD

ON THE BEACH IN BRAZIL

WHAT WE DID

- :: Purchased a two-year-old house in Trancoso, Brazil.

- :: Hired a New York attorney to research and verify the paperwork with the Brazilian consulate.

- :: Installed air conditioning.

- :: Built a small apartment above the garage for the young couple who manages the house year round. We couldn't do any of this without them. If you own a home abroad, there has to be someone to watch and take care of it while you are not there.

- :: Mixed in modern pieces with regional furniture that had been purchased from the previous owner.

- :: Laid at the pool while sipping Caipirinhas (Brazil's national cocktail) all day long.

FIRST STEPS

We have rented summer houses all over the world and every time we lose the deposit and usually get charged extra for damages. So, when a good friend of ours told us that he was selling a house that he'd built in Brazil, we were curious. We flew to Trancoso, a tiny town in Bahia, to take a look. We fell in love with the house and the town. Back in New York, Robert met with our attorney, who was a bit confused that we wanted to buy a house in Brazil. But he got over it, and proceeded to work with the Brazilian consulate making certain that everything was in order.

Financially, the house has turned out to be a great decision. During our first visit we stayed at a local hotel, which was as expensive as a hotel in St. Tropez. But we soon realized the price of the Brazil house was a tenth of what you would pay for one in St. Tropez. We bought this house and the one in Great Barrington combined for less than what you would pay for a one-bedroom house in the Hamptons. And the rental income the Brazil house produces pays for both mortgages.

MAKING YOUR HOUSE RENTER FRIENDLY

:: Provide a nanny (or at least information on where to find one), cleaning people, and as much other help as required.

:: Have great amenities: Our house includes high-speed Internet, satellite television, a library, music, movies and games, toys, surfboards, golf clubs, a dune buggy, an outdoor bar, and a pool table.

:: Make the house kid friendly but be sure not to clutter it with personal items.

:: Have air conditioning, particularly if your house is in warm climes.

:: Provide transportation from the airport with a car service or limo company.

:: Go out of your way to make it an amazing experience for the renters—they will go home and tell their friends about it.

When we told our friends and family that we bought a place in Brazil, they told us we were crazy. Everybody said there was crime there, or so they thought. In fact, there is little to no crime in Trancoso. The warnings about crime reminded me about my move to New York City. My friends from the South who visited were petrified to go into Central Park (even in daylight) because they thought they'd never come out alive. Turns out those stories about the city were exaggerated as well.

One of our family traditions is to sit around the dinner table every night and everyone tells his or her best part of the day. Usually, hearing their highlights is mine. So, dinner tables are pretty important in our homes. The table here was locally fabricated from refurbished wood. Whenever we have a piece of furniture we want to make, we bring our Brazilian carpenters pictures from magazines and they replicate the piece for a fraction of the cost. In most cases, their work has looked better than the original.

Beyond the kitchen and dining room, we added modern pieces to the otherwise natural décor. The mahogany throughout gives the home an earthy, very warm feel. We brought most of the modern pieces in suitcases from New York. We add a little more each time we come.

Because the house is great for kids, we are able to rent to families. We learned many kids ago to keep the art out of harm's way and to make things as indestructible as possible.

K.I.S.S:
KEEP IT SIMPLE SILLY

Every time we rented houses, we would move the breakable and expensive items out of the kids' reach. We actually would spend quite a while searching the place and remove almost everything that we thought would be susceptible to damage. When we finally had a rental property of our own, we made it as simple for the renters as possible: open spaces with no breakables in sight. If you have art on the walls, it must be framed. As for the décor, all the rooms have a clean, crisp look—this certainly went with the theme of a beach house and we didn't want anything too fussy.

When people rent they don't want to feel like they are in someone else's house—they want to feel like they are in a hotel. We designed the house to be elegant yet minimal, creating a relaxed and clean look.

"I dislike feeling at home when I'm abroad ..."

—GEORGE BERNARD SHAW

We have family soccer games every night.
When we travel, the kids become a lot closer to
one another because they don't have all of the
distractions they do when they are home.

"Travel is fatal to prejudice, bigotry, and narrow-mindedness."

—MARK TWAIN

Every time we are here, the kids spend a day at the local school learning a little Portuguese and they in turn teach the local children a little English. The more we go to Brazil, the more our kids have gained an understanding of the people and the culture. The education that they get while traveling is as good as they'll ever get in any school.

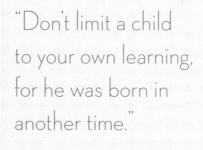

"Don't limit a child to your own learning, for he was born in another time."

—RABBINICAL SAYING

A neighbor brought these great whale bones to our front yard. The kids love them—it's like having a Museum of Natural History at the base of our driveway.

:: CHAPTER EIGHT

"Ask your child what he
wants for dinner
only if he's buying."

—FRAN LEBOWITZ

DECORATING
KIDS' ROOMS

THE
GIRLS'
ROOM

Our kids are still young, which means that for the most part we have a say in what their rooms look like. We know it won't last; soon pages from *Tiger Beat* will be taped to the walls along with pop star posters and other preteen treasures. That said, the kids love what we've done with their rooms—they're a little grown-up but still very much places where they can play, study, hang out, and feel like kids.

Our two girls share this room, which we decided should have lots of layers of pinks and purples. The antique beds from Bali came from ABC Home and Carpet. We got them for 50 percent off because they were floor samples. We bought the pink chairs at a garage sale for $20 and had them reupholstered, and the colorful floor covering came from the Rug Company.

> "Fashion fades.
> Style is
> eternal."
>
> —YVES SAINT LAURENT

THE BOYS' ROOM

We have four boys, and they all sleep in the same room. The two youngest are in facing cribs and the bigger boys' beds are right next to them. At a certain age, I am sure they won't like it anymore, but right now they really enjoy being all together.

When we moved into this house, we got rid of a lot of clutter and kept the spaces as open and comfortable as possible. Having fewer pieces of furniture also makes for a better flow. We positioned our paintings in places that the kids couldn't damage them. The art and the photos that are within their reach are framed with either glass or Plexiglas. We built cabinets in the playroom to store toys and gear, leaving the play area for them to go at it. We purposefully set up the bedrooms with play, study, and sleeping areas. At the end of the day, it's just a house with a bunch of stuff inside of it. The kids are what is important. Of course, our kids all know that if they break or destroy anything they will be sent to either military school or a nunnery!

As we do in rooms for adults, we mixed one-of-a-kind vintage pieces throughout and used oversize contemporary art as the focal point. We installed stainless steel baseboards, high hats, and light switches.

For the boys' bathroom, we built a Corian enclosure around an inexpensive tub, giving it a sleek look. The light is from Design Within Reach, one of our favorite stores. Lamps above bathtubs are illegal, as we have mentioned before, so this one is just decorative.

"A house is a
machine
for living."

—LE CORBUSIER

People often ask us how four boys can all share one room. We laugh, because we both grew up in large families with very small houses. Robert and his six brothers and sisters shared one bathroom. Everyone managed to stay fairly clean—and very close.

We mixed new sheets of fiberglass with an inexpensive door for the bathroom. The colors change with the light throughout the day.

We incorporated the male and female symbols using Moroccan tiles. Our tile setter arranged the tiles on a board and attached it to the wall in four sections.

I came across this essay recently, and I think it sums up how we feel pretty succinctly:

According to today's regulators and bureaucrats, those of us who were kids in the 40s, 50s, 60s, 70s or even the early 80s, probably shouldn't have survived. Our baby cribs were covered with bright colored lead-based paint. We had no childproof lids on medicine bottles, doors, or cabinets, and when we rode our bikes, we had no helmets. (Not to mention the risks we took hitchhiking.)

As children, we would ride in cars with no seat belts or air bags. Riding in the back of a pickup truck on a warm day was always a special treat. We drank water from the garden hose and not from a bottle. Horrors! We ate cupcakes, bread and butter, and drank soda pop with sugar in it, but we were never overweight because we were always outside playing. We shared one soft drink with four friends, from one bottle, and no one actually died from this.

We would spend hours building our go-carts out of wood scraps and fruit crates and then rode down the hill, only to find out we forgot the brakes. After running into the bushes a few times, we learned to solve the problem. We would leave home in the morning and play all day, as long as we were back when the streetlights came on.

No one was able to reach us by cell phone. Unthinkable! We did not have Playstations, Nintendo 64, X-Boxes, no video games at all, no ninety-nine channels on cable, videotape movies, surround sound, personal cell phones, personal computers, or Internet chat rooms. We had neighborhood friends! We played dodge ball, and sometimes, the ball would really hurt. We played other games such as Kick the Can and Capture the Flag. We fell out of trees, got cut, and broke bones and teeth, and there were no lawsuits from these accidents. They were accidents. No one was to blame but us.

We had fights and punched each other and got black and blue and learned to get over it. We made up games with sticks and tennis balls and ate worms, and although we were told it would happen, we did not put out very many eyes, nor did the worms live inside us forever. We rode bikes or walked to a friend's home and knocked on the door, or rang the bell or just walked in. Little League had tryouts and not everyone made the team. Those who didn't had to learn to deal with disappointment.

Some of us weren't as smart as others, so we failed a grade and were held back to repeat the same grade. Horrors! Tests were not adjusted for any reason. Our actions were our own. Consequences were expected, no one to hide behind. The idea of a parent bailing us out if we broke the law was unheard of. They actually sided with the law. Imagine that! This generation has produced some of the best risk-takers and problem solvers and inventors, ever.

—ANONYMOUS

:: CHAPTER NINE

ART LESSONS:

DECORATING WITH ART

The cool reindeer painting is by Francisco Larios.

- Have an opinion; buy what you like and not what someone else likes.

- Art is an investment. The money that you spend should be relative to how much you know about the piece.

- Do your homework. Or be sure to read "The Emperor's New Clothes."

- Don't let arrogant dealers or gallery employees intimidate you. They are there to sell the art, and your money is as green as anyone else's.

- Go to a large fair—you will see an a lot of art from all over the world in a short period of time.

- Go to see art at galleries and museums as often as possible. And ask questions of guides and lecturers.

- Take chances on young and little-known artists; the work is much more affordable.

Two years ago, we were visiting a friend's booth at the Art Basel fair in Miami Beach, and we witnessed one of the funniest things either of us had ever seen. Our friend, who wasn't selling anything for under $20,000, was approached by a woman who wanted to know how much his tape measure cost, as she thought that it was "brilliant." He jokingly said $25,000 and she replied, "Would you take twenty-two?" She was embarrassed when he told her that it was just a tape measure that he used while building his booth.

We have been collecting contemporary art for about six years. Aside from knowing what we like, we didn't know much about the art world. Our first purchase was *The Queen* by Ann Carrington (previous page), which Robert bought at a vintage clothing store for the price of an expensive suit. A year later we saw a similar piece by the same artist in *Vogue*. We knew that we had gotten a good deal. Since then, we've become addicted to collecting art from auctions, galleries, and art fairs.

The art world can be daunting, confusing, and intimidating. In the short time that we've been collecting, we've been lucky to have some wonderful people around to educate us.

"Painting is a faith,
and it imposes the duty to disregard public opinion."

—VINCENT VAN GOGH

Remember that you don't have to buy art in a gallery; there are plenty of other places to score great pieces. Artist Linda Mason painted these portraits of our daughters (top left). The flowers installation was a display for an Italian furniture show and cost next to nothing (left). Robert "won" the vintage Len Bias photograph on eBay (top right).

"There are no rules for good photographs.

There are only good photographs."

— ANSEL ADAMS

USING ART YOU ALREADY OWN

:: Frame a bunch of old black-and-white photos and cover a wall with them—we've done that in several of the houses we've designed and it looks great. Don't worry if you only have color photos: it's cheap to convert color photos to black and white.

:: Kids' paintings and drawings when framed and hung are a fun addition to any room.

:: Old travel posters and maps can be very impressive when on a wall, and they are inexpensive.

:: Kitschy flea market oil paintings can be cool in the right setting.

:: Blow up your favorite photos and frame them for a dramatic statement or turn them into wallpaper.

"Every child is an artist.

The problem is how to remain an artist once he grows up."

— PABLO PICASSO

This "installation" by Jan Eleni is one of the coolest things we have—and it was very inexpensive. She shrunk our kids' art and affixed it to a large piece of white board. People gravitate to this piece more than any of our other art. Many of our friends who are art aficionados ask us if it was done by a well-known artist—they are always a little embarrassed when we tell them it's by our kids.

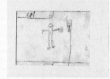

SEASONS GREETINGS

HOMEMADE HOLIDAY CARDS

Our interest in art and design has been a catalyst for one of our annual family projects: homemade holiday cards. We started this when Wolfie was born and have more and more fun with it every year. Year One: Pictures of us in a K-mart photo booth (opposite far left). Year Two: We moved the babies around on a black blanket until we got this great shot (opposite top). Year Three: We asked the photographer to take close-ups of the kids' eyes (opposite middle). Year Four: A collage of keepsakes and photographs from 2000—we laid them out and had them scanned (opposite bottom). Year Five: This was taken right after 9/11. Our friend Linda Mason painted the kids into an American flag (above).

Year Six: The kids added their artwork to this photo taken in St. Tropez when we were on vacation (top left). Year Seven: This time, Linda Mason painted the kids with Day-Glo paint and we shot the picture in the garage with black lights. It reads "Peace," a comment on the war in Iraq (above). Year Eight: I was five months pregnant with our second set of twins, Five and Holleder. The inside of the card reads, "Count your blessings" (top right).

Year Nine: Inspired by "Silent Night" (above left). Year Ten: A family photo from Brazil. We added the tree in Photoshop to give it a comic-book look (top right). Year Eleven: Enchanted. We took pictures of the kids and Photoshopped berries and flowers into them (top left). Year Twelve: From our home to yours (above right).

"Did anyone ever have a boring dream?"

—RALPH HODGSON

As always, we are on to the next thing. Currently, we are building a glass house on the West Side Highway in Manhattan as well as designing the first boutique hotel on the New Jersey shore. We count our blessings every day.

:: RESOURCES

Following is a brief selection of our favorite places to buy distinctive furnishings. Many of the items these shops carry can be on the expensive side, but most have sales, so good prices can be found. As you know already if you've read this book, we are addicted to flea markets and we go to as many as we can to scour for treasures. Amazing bargains can be had at flea markets—you just need to spend a little time looking. And we still love to shop for stuff at Ikea and Target: cool designs at rock-bottom prices. But if you are in the mood to splurge, the shops listed below are the place to go.

BOFFI
31 1/2 GREENE STREET
NEW YORK, NY 10012
TEL: 212 431 8282
WWW.BOFFI.COM

Boffi is a high-end retailer of Italian kitchens and bathrooms. They have locations around the country and other retailers also carry their products. Consult their Web site for more information.

GERVASI/WEST
968 SOUTH MAIN STREET
GREAT BARRINGTON, MA 01230
TEL: 413 528 9020
GERVASIWEST@YAHOO.COM

This is our favorite antiques store outside of Europe. Caroline, the owner, has an amazing eye and great deals. Now that we've recommended it, can we ask you not to go? We want all the good stuff for us!

HOMEWORKS
480 BROOME STREET
NEW YORK, NY 10013
TEL: 212 343 9900
WWW.HOMEWORKSNY.COM

This store has an extensive selection of custom window treatments, from drapes to shades. They also reupholster furniture.

KARTELL
39 GREENE STREET
NEW YORK, NY 10013
TEL: 212 966 6665
WWW.KARTELLUS.COM

Kartell makes cool modern furniture, and we are always able to find something interesting there. We often buy floor samples and save as much as 50% off the retail price. Be sure to ask the salespeople about this.

MOSAIC HOUSE
62 WEST 22ND STREET
NEW YORK, NY 10010
TEL: 212 414 2525
WWW.MOSAICHSE.COM

The have extraordinary handmade tiles from Morocco. Ask for Ben, the owner. For five generations, the men in Ben's family have been making tile. He is very helpful and creative. Plan on spending some time there—Ben is quite the talker!

MOSS
150 GREENE STREET
NEW YORK, NY 10012
TEL: 212 204 7100
WWW.MOSSONLINE.COM

Moss has an amazingly well-edited selection of interesting products, including lighting, furniture, and kitchen implements from around the world from cutting-edge designers. It feels very much like a museum because of the quality and uniqueness of what they sell, but of course you can touch everything!

NEVEN AND NEVEN MODERNE
618 WARREN STREET
HUDSON, NY 12534
TEL: 518 828 4214

This is a one-of-a-kind modern furnishings store in Hudson. Scott, the owner, has great taste and always is on the hunt for unique pieces from Cappellini to Starke. Hudson is a fun and quick 90-minute trip from New York City.

OLDE GOOD THINGS
124 WEST 24TH STREET
NEW YORK, NY 10011
TEL: 212 989 8401
WWW.OLDEGOODTHINGS.COM

We have bought some of our most distinctive vintage artifacts here, everything from fireplace mantels to chandeliers. Be sure to ask if there is something specific you want and can't find—they are happy to point you in the right direction. Don't miss the clearance area for rugs in the basement. There are literally thousands to choose from so make sure you have some time because they have beautiful goods at discount prices.

RUG COMPANY
88 WOOSTER STREET
NEW YORK, NY 10012
TEL: 212 274 0444

This U.K.-based purveyor has an extraordinary selection of unique rugs.

IF YOU ARE IN FRANCE

NICE FLEA MARKET
COURS SALEYA, BETWEEN THE OLD TOWN AND QUAI DES ETATS-UNIS
NICE, FRANCE

Somehow we always manage to get lost when trying to find the market, which only sells antiques on Mondays. Be sure not to drink too many rosés at the cafés that surround the market—otherwise you buy stuff you really don't want!

:: PHOTO CREDITS

l=left; r=right; t=top; m=middle; b=bottom

David Beyda: 164tr and mr

Corbis: 35t

Roberto D'Addona: 1, 8, 261, 37, 44, 57–58, 60–61, 64–65, 73, 85–87, 98–101, 132–34, 135r, 136–37, 140–41, 142–43t and b, 173

John Gruen: 67, 70–71, 79

Chris Hannan: 23, 28, 32–33, 38–43, 46–47, 106, 124b, 154–55, 166b

Dean Kaufman: 92–93, 124tl, 128, 156–57, 168–69

Linda Mason: 165, 167tl

Dan Mayers: 45, 54–56, 59

Joshua McHugh: 5, 19b, 24–25, 27, 29, 34, 35b, 50–53, 66, 68–69, 72, 81, 84, 89–91, 95, 98–102, 103r, 105, 107, 109–113, 117–21, 123, 124tr, 152–53, 163, 167br

Elizabeth Novogratz: 167tr

Robert Novogratz: 12–18, 19t, 22, 31, 36, 49, 63, 80, 162, 164br, 166tl

Costas Picadas: 74–76, 78, 82–83, 122r, 126–27, 145–47, 151, 159, 160–61

Nicole Marie Polec: 47r

Luc Roymans: 2, 21, 26r, 94, 96–97, 103l, 104, 130–31, 135l, 138–39, 143m

Anson Smart: 122l, 129, 149, 174

Bico Stupakoff: 114–16, 125, 148, 150

ACKNOWLEDGMENTS

Thanks to: our editor Isabel Venero, who gave us our big break;
Joshua McHugh and all the photographers who contributed
to this book; Chris Hannan for all his help during the many
stages before and during the making of the book;
and especially Elizabeth Novogratz, who wrote the text with us.